NEW HAMPSHIRE

Past and Present

Lauren Ciarleglio

rosen publishing's
rosen central

New York

To my parents

Published in 2011 by The Rosen Publishing Group, Inc.
29 East 21st Street, New York, NY 10010

Library of Congress Cataloging-in-Publication Data

Ciarleglio, Lauren.
New Hampshire : past and present / Lauren Ciarleglio. — 1st ed.
     p. cm. — (The United States: past and present)
Includes bibliographical references and index.
ISBN 978-1-4358-9489-1 (library binding) —
ISBN 978-1-4358-9516-4 (pbk. book) —
ISBN 978-1-4358-9550-8 (6-pack)
1. New Hampshire—Juvenile literature. I. Title.
CURR   F34.3.C53 2011
974.2—dc22

2009053334

Manufactured in Malaysia

CPSIA Compliance Information: Batch #S10YA: For further information, contact Rosen Publishing, New York, New York, at 1-800-237-9932.

On the cover: Top left: Early settlers arrive on the shore of New Hampshire. Top right: A shipyard in Portsmouth. Bottom: An autumn view of New England's highest point, Mount Washington.

Contents

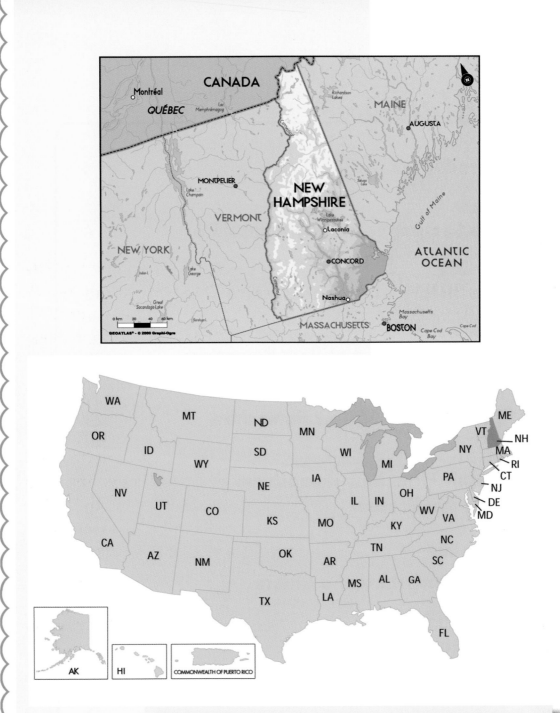

Located in the northeastern United States, New Hampshire is the nation's forty-sixth largest state. It is bordered by Canada, Maine, Vermont, Massachusetts, and the Atlantic Ocean. The state capital is Concord.

Introduction

New Hampshire is located in the northeastern United States. One of the six New England states, New Hampshire is bordered by Quebec, Canada, to the north, Maine to the east, Massachusetts to the south, and Vermont to the west. Triangular in shape, New Hampshire is about 180 miles (290 kilometers) from north to south and, at its widest point, stretches about 93 miles (150 km) from east to west. It is the forty-sixth largest state in the United States, with an area of 9,351 square miles (24,219 square km).

As one of the original thirteen colonies, New Hampshire has played an important part in American history. It was the first state to declare itself free from England and the first state to ratify the U.S. Constitution in 1776. New Hampshire was also home to the fourteenth president of the United States, Franklin Pierce. Today, New Hampshire continues to play a crucial role in this country's state of affairs. It has a unique government, including the largest legislative body of any state. It also holds the first presidential primary election in the nation.

Home to Mount Washington, the tallest peak in the Northeast, New Hampshire thrives on tourism. Visitors travel to the state throughout the year to enjoy its beautiful natural scenery, which includes numerous lakes and snow-capped mountains. New Hampshire has always valued independence, and the people who live there are proud of their state.

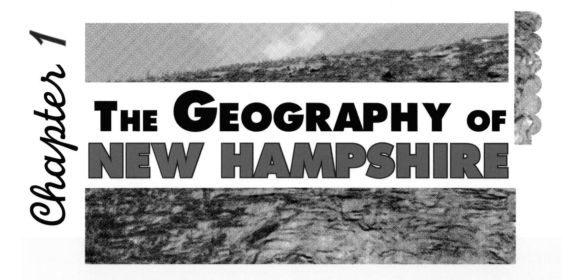

Chapter 1

THE GEOGRAPHY OF NEW HAMPSHIRE

New Hampshire is a mountainous state that has abundant forests, clear lakes, and a short coastline in the east of the state. Geographically, New Hampshire is part of the Appalachian Highlands. The state can be divided into three main regions: the Coastal Lowlands, the Eastern New England Uplands, and the White Mountain Region.

The Coastal Lowlands

New Hampshire's Coastal Lowlands are located in the southeastern part of the state, where there is a short 13-mile (21-km) coastline. Despite the fact that New Hampshire has the smallest sea coast of any state in the country, the coastline is a major tourist attraction. Located at a place where the Piscataqua River empties into the Atlantic Ocean, the city of Portsmouth is home to a large seaport and shipbuilding center. Portsmouth is also one of the nation's oldest cities, and features many historic buildings. Six miles (9.7 km) off the coast, in Piscataqua Bay, one can find the Isles of Shoals. Consisting of nine islands, the Isle of Shoals is named for the schools of fish in the surrounding ocean.

The city of Portsmouth features a large seaport and harbor. Located along New Hampshire's short coastline, it has served as an important shipping center over the years.

The Eastern New England Upland

The Eastern New England Upland makes up most of the state. The upland can be divided into three major areas: the Merrimack Valley, the Hills and Lakes Region, and the Connecticut River Valley.

The Merrimack Valley extends from the Massachusetts border to central New Hampshire. It is home to the state's three largest cities: Concord, Manchester, and Nashua.

Most of New Hampshire's freshwater lakes and ponds can be found in the Hills and Lakes Region. The largest lake in New

Hampshire, Lake Winnipesaukee, is located in this area. One out of thousands of lakes found in the state, Lake Winnipesaukee stretches for almost 80 square miles (207 sq km). The Hills and Lakes Region is located above the Coastal Lowlands and the Merrimack Valley, but it does not quite reach all the way to the Vermont border.

The Connecticut River Valley runs north to south along the Connecticut River, stretching to the Vermont border on the western side of the state. The valley is characterized by fertile land and lush forests.

The White Mountains

New Hampshire's third major geological region is the White Mountains, which are found in the north of the state. The White Mountains were named for their white-tipped peaks. Between the mountains, there are narrow valleys and forests.

The White Mountains Region is home to Mount Washington. This is the highest point in the northeastern United States, with an elevation of 6,288 feet (1,917 meters) above sea level. It is the largest of the mountains in the Presidential Range, all of which are named after former U.S. presidents. The others include Mount Madison, Mount John Adams, Mount John Quincy Adams, Mount Jefferson, Mount Monroe, Mount Pierce, and Mount Eisenhower.

Rivers and Lakes

There are five major rivers that run through the state of New Hampshire. The Connecticut River is the longest river in the state; it originates from several lakes to the north. The Merrimack River flows south into Massachusetts. The Androscoggin and Saco rivers drain from the White Mountains into Maine. The fifth major river in the state is the Piscataqua, which flows into the Atlantic Ocean.

New Hampshire's Lakes Region features many of the state's most pristine bodies of water. Lake Winnepesaukee is famous for being New Hampshire's largest lake, but there are many others. At the foot of the White Mountains is a collection of lakes known as the Squam Lakes. The largest of these lakes is simply known as Squam Lake, and it features a number of small islands. It is the state's second largest lake. The Squam Lakes also include Little Squam Lake and White Oak Pond.

Part of New Hampshire's White Mountains, Mount Washington is the highest point in New England.

Climate

The weather in New Hampshire is typical for New England. Summers are humid and warm. Winters are cold and wet, with an average snowfall of 60 to 100 inches (152 to 254 centimeters). The state's monthly temperatures range from an average high of 82.6 degrees Fahrenheit (28.1 degrees Celsius) in the summer to an average low of 9°F (-12.8°C) in the winter. The highest recorded temperature is 106°F (41°C) in 1911, and the lowest recorded temperature is -47°F (-44°C) in 1934.

Changes to the Land

For several centuries, human activity has caused the landscape in New Hampshire to undergo significant changes. When European colonists first settled on the land in the seventeenth century, they began to cut down trees. The colonists also began hunting on land that belonged to New Hampshire's Native American residents, the Abenaki. The effects that the colonists had on the land greatly disrupted the Abenaki way of life.

Over the years, the state's population grew exponentially. As a result, development continued. The Industrial Revolution changed New Hampshire in the early nineteenth century. Factories and mills sprang up throughout the state, contributing to air pollution. The state's forests continued to be cut down for timber. A number of dams were also built during this period.

Today, many of the dams that were built in New Hampshire during the Industrial Revolution no longer serve a purpose. The Department of Environmental Services is currently considering removing some of these dams. Removing the dams would improve water quality, and restore plant and animal habitats in New Hampshire's rivers.

New Hampshire's government is careful to take good care of the state's environment. The state's industries and utilities are among the most environmentally friendly in the country. However, New Hampshire is not entirely pollution-free. Much of the state's pollution comes from vehicle emissions, which contribute to air pollution. To counter this, there are programs such as the Granite State Clean Cities Coalition that focus on reducing transportation emissions and promoting low-emission fuel alternatives. The New Hampshire Department of Environmental Services encourages residents to take action to protect their state's environment.

Plant and Animal Life

About 80 percent of New Hampshire is covered in forests. These forests are made up of many different kinds of trees. Some of the most common trees found in the state are birch, hemlock, maple, oak, spruce, and white pine. In the fall, the splendor of the turning foliage makes New Hampshire a major tourist attraction. Thousands of people travel to the state to see its forests turn shades of red, orange, and yellow. Flowers such as goldenrod, pink-lady slippers, purple lilacs, rhododendron, and violets grow throughout New Hampshire, and various kinds of alpine flowers flourish in the mountains.

Moose can be found roaming the forests of New Hampshire. An adult moose can weigh up to 1,000 pounds (454 kilograms).

New Hampshire is home to mammals small and large, such as beavers, black bears, brown bears, chipmunks, raccoons, and white-tailed deer. Although rare, moose can be spotted in New Hampshire's forests. The state is also home to a variety of birds, such as blue jays, robins, sparrows, and woodpeckers, as well as game birds like ducks, pheasants, and wild turkeys. Fish, including bass, catfish, eel, and salmon, thrive in the state's many lakes and ponds.

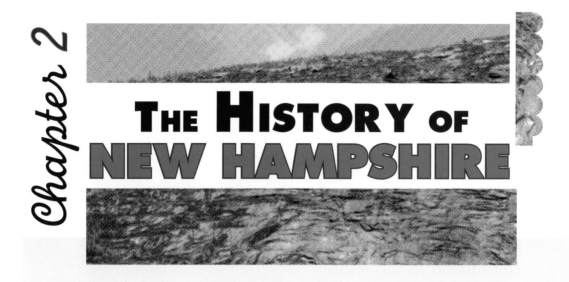

Chapter 2

THE HISTORY OF NEW HAMPSHIRE

Long before the United States was a country, Native Americans lived in the area that is now known as New Hampshire. Most Native Americans in New Hampshire belonged to tribes that are collectively referred to as the Abenaki. The Abenaki were part of a larger nation of tribes called the Algonquin.

The Algonquin tribes got along well. They joined forces to fight against their rivals, the Iroquois Indians of northern New York. In New Hampshire, the Abenaki farmed the land and grew crops such as beans, corn, and squash. They also hunted and fished for food. Trading among the Abenaki tribes and communities was part of their daily life. Today, many towns and cities in New Hampshire still carry names that the state's Native Americans gave them.

Exploration and Colonization

In the early 1600s, European explorers began arriving in New Hampshire. French explorer Samuel de Champlain became one of the first Europeans to explore New England. De Champlain sailed along the Piscataqua River, which runs through New Hampshire. Another European explorer, Captain John Smith, sailed along the East Coast and visited the Isles of Shoals off the New Hampshire shoreline.

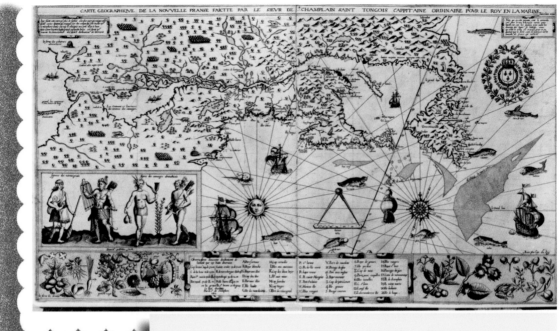

CARTE GEOGRAPHIQVE DE LA NOVVELLE FRANSE FAICTE PAR LE SIEVR DE CHAMPLAIN SAINT TONGOIS CAPPITAINE ORDINAIRE POVR LE ROY EN LA MARINE

Samuel de Champlain was one of the first European explorers to interact with Native Americans living in New England. This early seventeenth-century map details his voyages to America.

In the 1620s, European settlers began arriving in New England. In 1622, King James I of England granted John Mason, a former governor of Newfoundland, Canada, and Sir Ferdinando Gorges, a former military governor of Plymouth, England, a large piece of land in New England. Seven years later, the two men decided to divide this land. Gorges took the section to the east, which became Maine. Mason took the land between the Merrimack and Piscataqua rivers. He named this land New Hampshire, after the county of Hampshire in England, where he came from.

The French and Indian War

As more and more British settlers began to make New Hampshire their permanent home, the Native Americans there began to feel threatened. They were afraid that they would be forced off of the land. Soon, a war broke out between the colonists and Native Americans. Many Native American tribes throughout the Northeast, including the New Hampshire Abenaki tribes, formed an alliance with the French. The French wanted to drive the British out of North America and take over the land.

The French and Indian War lasted from 1754 to 1763, when the French signed the Treaty of Paris. This treaty gave all of the colonies in Canada to the British. Soon after, many of New Hampshire's Native Americans fled to Canada to avoid further attacks from the British. By the eighteenth century, few Native Americans were left in the state.

The American Revolution

After the conflict with the French ended, the British colonists turned their attention to a different issue. During this time, the thirteen colonies spoke out against Britain's Parliament, which governed the colonists from afar and levied taxes against them. Even though the colonists paid taxes, they did not have any representatives in Parliament. They felt that this situation was not fair. They believed that Britain was too far away from the colonies to effectively govern them. The colonists declared their independence from Britain, resulting in the Revolutionary War.

The first military action of the Revolutionary War occurred in New Hampshire in 1774. At this time, John Sullivan, a military

This painting depicts New Hampshire General John Stark fighting the British at the Battle of Bennington during the Revolutionary War.

officer who later became New Hampshire's governor, led a group of colonists in a raid on Fort William and Mary on the island of New Castle. Sullivan and the colonists took control of British weapons and supplies inside the fort. These weapons are believed to have been used by New Hampshire soldiers at the Battle of Bunker Hill in Boston, Massachusetts, just a few months later.

In 1777, General John Stark of New Hampshire led the colonists to victory over the British at the Battle of Bennington. Stark became famous for providing New Hampshire with its state motto, "Live Free or Die."

Education in New Hampshire

Education in New Hampshire has evolved over the years. In the early 1600s, the state enforced public education in all towns of fifty homes or more. And in 1769, New Hampshire's famous Dartmouth College was founded by Reverend Eleazar Wheelock. Throughout the 1800s, larger towns divided into districts, and each district had its own school. Districts voted on school superintendents, and town meetings were held to raise money. School boards were elected to represent their school systems.

During this period, New Hampshire opened its first public high school in Portsmouth. By the end of the century, more than 2,200 school districts existed in the state.

Today, New Hampshire's educational system is firmly in place. The New Hampshire Department of Education is committed to providing education to every New Hampshire resident. The department is responsible for enforcing all aspects of educational law, leadership, and development in every New Hampshire community. Originally, mandatory attendance laws enforced school attendance for children up to the age of fourteen. But today, attending high school is compulsory for children up to sixteen. New Hampshire's state government is solely responsible for providing educational funds, which are raised through property taxes.

There are now more than forty colleges and universities in New Hampshire. These institutions include the University of New Hampshire, Southern New Hampshire University, Plymouth State University, and Keene State College. An Ivy League school, Dartmouth College is the oldest college in the state and one of the ten oldest in the United States. It is considered to be one of the best colleges in the country.

When the Revolutionary War ended in 1781, New Hampshire became the first state to adopt its own constitution and form an independent government. In 1788, it became the ninth state to ratify the U.S. Constitution and the ninth state to join the new country. The state capital was first established in Portsmouth, but it was later moved to Concord.

The Civil War

By the nineteenth century, southern states in America were dependent on slavery, a practice that was banned in the north. John Dickson, a congressman from Keene, New Hampshire, was the first politician to ever speak out against slavery in front of the U.S. Congress. Many people wanted slavery to be abolished throughout the entire United States. In hopes of keeping tensions over the issue of slavery from splitting the country apart, Daniel Webster, another New Hampshire native who opposed slavery, proposed the Compromise of 1850. This law allowed the South to use slave labor, which would remain illegal in the North. Passed into law in order to prevent war from breaking out between the North and the South, the compromise was broken a few years later in 1854, when the Kansas-Nebraska Act was passed.

A New Hampshire native and abolitionist, Moses Sawyer helped runaway slaves escape to Canada through the Underground Railroad.

17

This nineteenth-century millhouse is located along the Squamscott River. Toward the end of the 1800s, industry expanded in New Hampshire, and factories and mills employed many New Hampshire citizens.

The Kansas-Nebraska Act allowed people in these territories to vote on whether or not to allow slavery.

At this time, the Underground Railroad, a secret network of routes and safe houses, came into existence. The Underground Railroad helped slaves escape to the North. There were several Underground Railroad stops throughout New Hampshire, and many state residents who were opposed to slavery did what they could to help runaway slaves escape even farther north to Canada, where slavery was illegal.

In the spring of 1861, the southern states seceded from the rest of the country. On April 12, 1861, war broke out between the North and the South. Approximately thirty-five thousand New Hampshire men fought in the Civil War, and about five thousand were killed in the fighting. The North won the war in 1865.

In the years following the Civil War, industry in New Hampshire began expanding. Factories began to replace farms. By the 1870s, manufacturing jobs employed more than half of New Hampshire's residents. Textile manufacturing was the most prominent industry in the state. Immigrants began arriving in New Hampshire in the early twentieth century to work in the textile mills. They came from European countries such as France, Ireland, and Poland. Many immigrants also came from parts of Canada.

Twentieth-Century New Hampshire

During World War I, which lasted from 1914 to 1918, New Hampshire's factories made clothing, weapons, and ships for the U.S. military. In 1929, the U.S. stock market crashed, sending the country into a severe economic crisis known as the Great Depression. When the Great Depression hit, many New Hampshire residents lost their jobs. Thousands were unable to find work.

In 1939, World War II began. The United States entered the war in 1941. The demand for ships, submarines, and uniforms meant that New Hampshire residents were able to once again find work in the state's factories. Approximately sixty thousand New Hampshire civilians served in the armed forces during World War II.

Chapter 3

THE GOVERNMENT OF NEW HAMPSHIRE

New Hampshire prides itself on its unique government, which includes a large body of representatives known as a citizen legislature. The state has a great deal of influence on the nation's politics, as it holds the first nationwide political party primary elections in the country. New Hampshire's government is divided into three branches: the executive branch, the legislative branch, and the judicial branch. The state capitol building is in the city of Concord, which is in the center of the state.

The Executive Branch

New Hampshire's executive branch is unique in that it consists of both a governor and a five-member executive council. The governor works with the executive council to enforce the laws of the state. The members of the council have an equal share in the governor's responsibilities. They also have the right to veto the governor. Each council member represents a different segment of the state's population, and each has a full-time career outside of politics. Together, the governor and the executive council are in charge of nominating and appointing people, such as commissioners and judges, to state agencies.

New Hampshire state legislators gather at the State House in Concord in 2000. New Hampshire has the largest state legislative body in the United States, with around four hundred members.

They also appoint the state's attorney general. The governor and the members of the executive council serve two-year terms.

The Legislative Branch

The state's legislative branch, also called the general court, consists of the house of representatives and the senate. New Hampshire's house of representatives is the largest state legislative body in the United States. In fact, the only legislative body that outnumbers it in the United States is the U.S. Congress. At one time, New Hampshire's

Taxes in New Hampshire

Heavy taxes were one of the reasons why the colonies struggled to be free of British rule. In fact, the slogan "No taxation without representation" was frequently used by the colonists to express their grievance with the taxes levied against them by the British. After winning its independence, the young United States had few taxes, and no state had income taxes.

During the Civil War, the federal government began taxing peoples' income to help pay for the war effort. The Revenue Act of 1861 became the United States' first income tax law. People who made more than $800 a year had to pay income tax. Over the years, the nation's tax laws changed many times. Different states enacted different systems of taxation. The voters of New Hampshire chose to remain largely free of taxes.

Today, New Hampshire is one of the only states that does not have an individual income tax or general sales tax. However, the state's property taxes are among the highest in the country. Money for education is raised through property taxes. Some residents believe that a state income tax should be created to help fund schools. This has become a highly controversial topic throughout the state, as many New Hampshire residents take pride in having no income tax and strongly believe that the state is better off without it. The state government takes the tax system that exists in New Hampshire very seriously. In fact, newly elected governors traditionally make a vow that they will not raise taxes in the state, or suggest new ones.

New Hampshire's limited taxes attract many businesses to the state. According to the New Hampshire Business Resource Center, the state has the eighth-best business tax environment in the country. In addition to property taxes, New Hampshire also has taxes on hotels and cars and collects highway tolls.

house of representatives grew to 443 members. But the decision was made to limit membership to no more than 400 representatives and no fewer than 375. Each member that joins the house typically is not a full-time politician; representatives only earn about $200 per two-year term, making it impossible for the position to be their only source of income. Instead, they pursue careers outside of government as well.

The state senate has twenty-four members. The house and senate meet annually at the State House in Concord to hold elections and discuss bills. They also make sure that bills are publicly heard before a vote. Together, the house and senate write and vote on the laws that govern New Hampshire. When the governor is out of the state, the senate president takes his or her place, making any urgent decisions should the need arise.

The Judicial Branch

The judicial branch is comprised of the state's court system. The system is divided up into five main courts. The Supreme Court is the highest of these courts. It deals with issues that involve the state executives, the legislative branch, and the federal courts. There are five justices, or judges, on the New Hampshire Supreme Court.

The state's superior court handles civil lawsuits, custody cases, divorce cases, and felonies. The superior court is the only court where trials are held with a jury. Small lawsuits, such as landlord and tenant issues, instances of juvenile delinquency, and traffic violations are handled by the district court. Cases involving adoptions, name changes, real estate, and wills take place in the probate court. The family division court examines cases involving child abuse, child support, divorce, domestic violence, guardianship, and neglect.

Judges for all of the courts in the state of New Hampshire are nominated and appointed by the governor and the executive council.

The New Hampshire Primary

Every four years, New Hampshire holds the first presidential primary election in the country. Here, votes are tallied for the 2008 primary election.

Four people from New Hampshire represent the state in Congress: two senators and two representatives. As the location of the presidential primary election, New Hampshire has a significant influence on national politics. The primary election is held every four years. It helps determine which candidate each party will select to run for president of the United States in the general election. The very first primary election took place in New Hampshire on March 9, 1920. During the general election, or the presidential election, voting is opened up to the general public. New Hampshire has four electoral votes in the election.

Chapter 4

THE ECONOMY OF NEW HAMPSHIRE

Over the centuries, New Hampshire has seen its economy gradually shift. Once a heavily agricultural state, New Hampshire now has thriving manufacturing and technology industries. Even though the focus of the state economy has changed, New Hampshire's abundant forests still allow for the ample production of lumber and maple syrup. Fruits and vegetables are still grown by New Hampshire's farmers, and a number of dairy farms exist in the state as well. In addition, New Hampshire's striking mountains, lush forests, clear lakes, and charming oceanfront encourage a prosperous tourist industry.

Agriculture and Natural Resources

Today, agriculture only accounts for about 1 percent of New Hampshire's gross state product. Fewer than two thousand farms now exist in the state. Most of these are dairy farms, and they are generally found in the southern half of the state. New Hampshire's farms began disappearing when the cost of maintaining farmland became too great.

New Hampshire is covered in forests, and lumber is an important resource in the state. Cedar, pine, and spruce are often used to make

New Hampshire has a flourishing lumber industry. Timber is an important resource and is used for building homes and producing paper.

paper. Like its neighbor Vermont, New Hampshire produces quite a bit of maple syrup. Around 69,000 gallons (261,193 liters) of maple syrup are produced from sap taken from the state's maple trees every year. Crops such as corn and potatoes, and fruits such as apples, blueberries, and strawberries, are raised on the state's farms. Fishing also contributes to New Hampshire's economy, and along the coast fishermen catch cod, flounder, haddock, lobster, and shrimp. Fishing also takes place inland in the state's many lakes and ponds.

Industry, Manufacturing, and Technology

New Hampshire has few tax obligations, which attracts businesses to the state. Factories in New Hampshire create many products, including machinery, television equipment, software, medical equipment, and a variety of electronics. Leather is also manufactured in the state. Manchester, Portsmouth, and Nashua are New Hampshire's leading manufacturing cities. New Hampshire exports products all over the world. Machinery and computers make up most of the state's exports.

New Hampshire also has a sizable high-tech industry. Many people who are employed in New Hampshire's high-tech job sector hail from other states, such as New York and Massachusetts.

Tourism and Recreation

Tourism is one of New Hampshire's leading industries, bringing in billions of dollars each year. The state's mountains are home to many ski resorts and hiking trails, which draw thousands of visitors annually. Mount Washington, the highest peak in New England, is a state park. The mountain has a railway that allows visitors to tour it.

Lake Winnipesaukee is a major tourist attraction in the summertime. Many people flock to Lake Winnipesaukee to go boating, fishing, and swimming and to explore the lake's many small islands. New Hampshire's many other lakes are also popular with tourists, as are its state forests and parks. New Hampshire is home to what is known as the Oldest Summer Resort in America, in Wolfeboro. It is near Lake Winnepesaukee and has been a popular

Making a Living

The way people make their living in New Hampshire has changed over the years. Granite quarries used to be a huge industry in the state, employing a large workforce. However, the number of people employed in granite quarries has decreased, mainly due to the fact that materials such as concrete and steel are now used for most construction projects.

Farming also used to be crucial to the New Hampshire economy, but it began to decline in the mid-1800s. The state now has fewer than two thousand farms, which account for about 1 percent of the economy.

The Industrial Revolution provided new ways for people to make a living in New Hampshire. As the Civil War ended, factories and mills sprang up. Thousands of men, women, and even children were employed in positions at factories. During World War II, thousands of people were employed in the state's factories.

Today, the timber industry employs thousands of people in New Hampshire. The seacoast provides jobs for people in the fishing and shipping industry at the seaport. However, most people in New Hampshire make money in various manufacturing and technology jobs. Approximately eighty thousand New Hampshire citizens work in the manufacturing or technology industry. Many residents make a living in the service industry as doctors, lawyers, and salesclerks. New Hampshire's tourism and housing markets support the finance, insurance, and real estate industries.

Although New Hampshire has suffered from economic recessions throughout its history, the state has consistently been able to recover. During economic troubles, Hampshire's unemployment rate has repeatedly proven to be lower than the national average. The state continues to have a reputation as one of the best states to live and work in.

summer destination since the late 1700s.

Mount Monadnock is the most-climbed mountain in North America. Located southwest of Concord, it is the state's tallest mountain. Those who ascend to the peak of Mount Monadnock are treated to a breathtaking view. From the top of the mountain, all six New England states can be seen. During the fall, people travel to the state just to view the beautiful foliage.

New Hampshire is known for its beautiful landscape, which attracts tourists from all over the country.

Chapter 5

PEOPLE FROM NEW HAMPSHIRE:
PAST AND PRESENT

Many New Hampshire citizens have made valuable contributions to the state and to the country as a whole. These noteworthy leaders, politicians, artists, musicians, and writers have helped define what New Hampshire stands for today.

Josiah Bartlett (1729–1795) Josiah Bartlett played a major role in the early politics of the United States. After studying medicine, Bartlett became a physician in Kingston, New Hampshire. He entered politics in 1765 and would go on to represent New Hampshire in the Continental Congress. Bartlett was the second person to sign the Declaration of Independence. In 1782, Bartlett was appointed to the New Hampshire Supreme Court and became the chief justice in 1788. He would go on to become the first governor of New Hampshire.

Dan Brown (1964–) Born and raised in Exeter, New Hampshire, author Dan Brown has captured the world's attention with his best-selling novels. Brown's interest in conspiracy theories and history led him to write his two most famous books, *Angels and Demons* and *The Da Vinci Code*. These books were somewhat controversial due to their unique mixture of history, religion, and conspiracy theories. Both have been made into movies.

Dan Brown is the popular author of *The Da Vinci Code,* which is one of the best selling novels of all time.

Daniel Chester French (1850–1931) Born in Exeter, sculptor Daniel Chester French produced the famous Lincoln Memorial in Washington, D.C. The monument took many years to complete—in fact, it took six years to simply perfect the lighting on the sculpture, which draws thousands of tourists each year. French also created a sculpture called *The Minute Man*, commemorating a Revolutionary War battle that took place in Concord, Massachusetts, and a statue of George Washington on horseback in Paris, France.

Edward MacDowell (1860–1908) Edward MacDowell was a noteworthy composer and musician from Peterborough. After his death in 1908, his wife created the MacDowell Colony, where writers, musicians, and artists could be free to devote themselves to their work in solitude.

New Hampshire Writers

There has been a long tradition of talented writers in New Hampshire. Some have found the New Hampshire outdoors a great inspiration for their work, while others simply found the state to be a peaceful place to work.

Sarah Josepha Hale (1788–1879) was an important early American writer born in Newport, New Hampshire. She is most famous for her nursery rhyme "Mary Had a Little Lamb," along with other poetry. Hale was also a novelist and a leading editor of her time. New Hampshire native Thomas Bailey Aldrich (1836–1907) was a respected novelist, poet, and journalist during the late 1800s. The young character Tom Bailey in Aldrich's 1870 novel, *The Story of a Bad Boy*, is said to have influenced Mark Twain's creation of the character Tom Sawyer. The most famous writer to live in New Hampshire was the novelist and short story writer J. D. Salinger (1919–2010). His classic novel *The Catcher in the Rye* was published in 1951.

Today, many well-known writers continue to come from New Hampshire. Tomie dePaola (1934–) is an award-winning author and illustrator from New London. He is best known for his children's books. One of his most well-known books is *Brava, Strega Nona!*. Jodi Picoult is an award-winning novelist living in Hanover. She has written and published hundreds of books mostly about relationships, love, and family. Often, these books are based on her own life experiences. Picoult's novel *My Sister's Keeper* was made into a film in 2009. One of New Hampshire's most successful modern writers is Dan Brown (1964–), author of *The Da Vinci Code*.

Beginning in 1956, a prize known as the Sarah Josepha Hale Award has been given to writers who express their love of New England through their work. This annual award was first given to Pulitzer Prize–winning poet Robert Frost (1874–1963), who lived for a time in New Hampshire. Tomie dePaola won the award in 2007.

John Mason (1586–1635) John Mason was a British colonist who founded New Hampshire. He was given the land in 1629 and named it after the county he came from in England, Hampshire. Mason never had the chance to visit the new colony that he had been granted, nor did he ever get to see North America. At the time of his death 1635, he had been planning to make the voyage.

Christa McAuliffe (1948–1986) Christa McAuliffe was a Concord High School teacher chosen by the National Aeronautics and Space Administration (NASA) in 1985 to be the first private citizen in space. She was one of approximately eleven thousand teachers who applied to be a member of the space shuttle crew. She was killed when the *Challenger* space shuttle exploded soon after liftoff in 1986. McAuliffe had planned to travel around the country upon her return, giving lectures to students about her experience in space.

Bob Montana (1920–1975) Bob Montana was the creative mind behind the comic strip *Archie*, created in 1941. Montana based many of his comic strip characters on his Manchester High School classmates. He continued to draw Archie until his death in 1975.

Passaconaway (circa 1580–1666) A Native American chief and head of the Pennacook tribe, Passaconaway (meaning "child of the bear") was considered a great leader. He fought to keep peace with the European colonists as they settled in New Hampshire.

Jeanne Shaheen served as the first female governor of New Hampshire from 1997 to 2003. In 2008, she became the first woman from New Hampshire to be elected to the U.S. Senate.

Franklin Pierce (1804–1869) Born in Hillsboro, New Hampshire, Franklin Pierce was the fourteenth president of the United States, serving from 1853 to 1857. Prior to becoming president, Pierce served in the military and eventually became an established lawyer. He was forty-eight years old when he became president, making him the youngest person to hold that office at the time. His support of slavery made him so unpopular that he was not nominated for a second presidential term. After his presidency, Pierce returned to New Hampshire, where he resided with his wife, Jane Appleton Pierce.

J. D. Salinger (1919–2010) J. D. Salinger was an American novelist and short story writer. His most famous work is the 1951 novel *The Catcher in the Rye*, which is taught in schools all over the country. Salinger was extremely protective of his privacy and ceased publishing his writing in the 1960s. Born in New York City, he moved to Cornish, New Hampshire, in 1953.

Adam Sandler (1966–) Actor and comedian Adam Sandler grew up and attended high school in Manchester. After his stint as a featured performer in the television sketch-comedy show *Saturday Night Live*, Sandler went on to star in a number popular comedy films, such as *Billy Madison*, *Happy Gilmore*, and *The Wedding Singer*. He was nominated for a Golden Globe award for his performance in the 2002 film *Punch-Drunk Love*. Today, Sandler continues to work as an actor, comedian, and producer.

Jeanne Shaheen (1947–) The first woman to be elected governor of New Hampshire, Jeanne Shaheen served three two-year terms from 1997 to 2003. She focused on the state's school system, the needs of middle-class families, and the state economy. Shaheen is still active in New Hampshire politics.

Alan Shepard (1924–1998) Born in East Derry, Alan Shepard was the first American in space. During the 1971 Apollo 14 expedition, he became the fifth man to walk on the Moon. After landing on the Moon, he famously bounced around for the camera, and even hit golf balls into space.

John Stark (1728–1822) The man behind the state's motto, "Live Free or Die," John Stark fought to free New England from Great Britain. During the American Revolution, he led American forces to victory during the Battle of Bunker Hill as a military general. Considered a war hero, Stark is one of New Hampshire's most famous soldiers. After the Revolutionary War ended, he settled in Manchester with his wife, Molly, and his ten children.

Daniel Webster (1782–1852) Daniel Webster was a lawyer and statesman who openly spoke out against slavery. Despite this, he proposed a law called the Compromise of 1850, which allowed slavery to exist in the South but not in the North. He hoped this compromise would keep the country unified. Ultimately, it only served to postpone the Civil War. In 1812, Webster was elected to represent New Hampshire in

Daniel Webster was an important New Hampshire statesman and politician. He proposed the Compromise of 1850 in an attempt to keep peace between the North and South.

the U.S. House of Representatives. Although he never realized his dreams of becoming president, Webster played an important role in the U.S. government. Besides being a congressperson for New Hampshire, he was also a representative and a senator for Massachusetts. In addition, Webster served as secretary of state to three presidents.

Timeline

1623	The first colonial settlement is founded at Dover.
1629	John Mason takes the land given to him by the king of England and establishes New Hampshire.
1642	Children in New Hampshire are required to be taught reading, citizenship, and religion.
1769	Dartmouth College is founded by Reverend Eleazar Wheelock.
1774	New Hampshire becomes the first state to declare itself free from England.
1778	New Hampshire holds the first constitutional convention.
1788	New Hampshire becomes the ninth state to ratify the Constitution.
1800	The navy yard is established in Portsmouth.
1808	The state capital is established in Concord.
1830	The nation's first public high school is established in Portsmouth.
1833	The nation's first public library is established in Peterborough.
1853	New Hampshire native Franklin Pierce becomes the fourteenth president of the United States.
1920	The first primary election in a presidential election takes place.
1961	East Derry native Alan Shepard becomes the first American in space.
1986	Schoolteacher Christa McAuliffe is killed when the *Challenger* space shuttle explodes after liftoff.
1997	Jeanne Shaheen became the first woman governor of the state.
2001	New Hampshire's property tax becomes the primary source for school funding.
2002	Jeanne Shaheen is the first woman from New Hampshire to hold a seat in the U.S. Senate.
2009	New Hampshire legalizes same-sex marriage.

New Hampshire at a Glance

State motto:	"Live Free or Die"
State capital:	Concord
State flower:	Purple lilac
State bird:	Purple finch
State tree:	White birch
State animal:	White-tailed deer
State fruit:	Pumpkin
Statehood date and number:	June 21, 1788; ninth state
State nickname:	The Granite State
Total area and U.S. rank:	9,351 square miles (15,049 square km); forty-sixth largest state
Population:	1,316,000
Length of coastline:	13 miles (21 km)
Highest elevation:	Mount Washington, at 6,288 feet (1,917 m) above sea level
Lowest elevation:	Sea level, at the state's coastline

State Flag

State Seal

Major rivers:	Androscoggin River, Connecticut River, Merrimack River, Piscataqua River, Saco River
Major lakes:	Lake Winnipesaukee, Newfound Lake, Squam Lake
Highest temperature recorded:	106°F (41°C) at Nashua, July 4, 1911
Lowest temperature recorded:	-47° F (-44°C) on Mount Washington, January 29, 1934
Origin of state name:	From the English county of Hampshire
Chief agricultural products:	Apples, blueberries, corn, potatoes, strawberries
Major industries:	Electronics, finance, insurance, timber, tourism

Purple finch

Purple lilac

alliance An agreement among two or more groups to work together for a common good.

bill A proposed law that is discussed and voted on by the government.

colonist A person who settles in a land or country, but retains the customs, traditions, or government of their homeland.

depression A lengthy period during which a country's economy suffers, often resulting in widespread unemployment and poverty.

emissions Particles or energy released into the air.

export To send a product to another country in exchange for money.

felony A serious crime that is typically punished by imprisonment.

foliage The leaves of a plant, often a tree.

gross Income or profit before taxes are taken out.

Industrial Revolution A period during the eighteenth century when the economy changed drastically due to the spread of technology and manufacturing.

Ivy League A group of eight prestigious universities in the eastern United States.

juvenile delinquency Illegal or antisocial behavior performed by a young person.

levy To legally impose or collect a tax.

mandatory Something that is required.

primary election A preliminary election to select candidates for a presidential election.

quarry An open excavation site where stones, such as granite, are collected.

ratify To formally approve something.

secede To separate or withdraw from a larger establishment.

sketch comedy Short comedic scenes that are acted out by a performer or group of performers.

slavery The practice of forcing another person or a group of people, often by the threat of violence or death, to work in some capacity for the benefit of others.

solitude The act of being alone.

tax A fee imposed by the government on goods or services.

Underground Railroad A secret route established before the Civil War by which slaves escaped the South.

Canterbury Shaker Village

288 Shaker Road
Canterbury, NH 03224
(603) 783-9511
Web site: http://www.shakers.org
This organization maintains the historic Shaker village. The village also has tours and exhibits.

Franklin Pierce Homestead

P.O. Box 896
Hillsborough, NH 03244
(603) 478-3165
Web site: http://www.franklinpierce.ws/homestead/contents.html
This childhood home of the fourteenth president of the United States is open to the general public.

McAuliffe–Shepard Discovery Center

2 Institute Drive
Concord, NH 03301
(603) 271-7827
Web site: http://www.starhop.com
Named in memory of Christa McAuliffe and Alan Shepard, the McAuliffe-Shepard Discovery Center contains exhibits and programs to teach children science and the humanities.

Mount Washington Observatory

2779 White Mountain Highway
P.O. Box 2310
North Conway, NH 03860
(603) 356-2137
Web site: http://www.mountwashington.org
The mission of the observatory is to increase understanding of Earth's weather and provide information about Mount Washington.

New England Ski Museum

P.O. Box 267

Franconia, NH 03580

(603) 823-9505

Web site: http://www.skimuseum.org

The New England Ski Museum maintains exhibits on the history of skiing.

New Hampshire Audubon

84 Silk Farm Road

Concord, NH 03301

(603) 224-9909

Web site: http://www.nhaudubon.org

This nonprofit organization provides information on protecting New Hampshire's wildlife and environment.

New Hampshire Historical Society

6 Eagle Square

Concord, NH 03301

(603) 228-6688

Web site: http://www.nhhistory.org

This organization maintains both a library and a museum, which provide the general public with information on the history of the state of New Hampshire.

Web Sites

Due to the changing nature of Internet links, Rosen Publishing has developed an online list of Web sites related to the subject of this book. This site is updated regularly. Please use this link to access the list:

http://www.rosenlinks.com/uspp/nhpp

FOR FURTHER READING

DiConsiglio, John. *Franklin Pierce: America's 14th President.* New York, NY: Children's Press, 2004.

Feldman, Ruth Tenzer. *How Congress Works: A Look at the Legislative Branch.* Minneapolis, MN: Lerner Publications, 2004.

Haulley, Fletcher. *A Primary Source History of the Colony of New Hampshire.* New York, NY: Rosen Publishing Group, 2007.

Hicks, Terry Allan. *New Hampshire.* Tarrytown, NY: Marshall Cavendish Benchmark, 2005.

Kent, Deborah. *New Hampshire.* New York, NY: Children's Press, 2009.

Mattern, Joanne. *New Hampshire: The Granite State.* Strongsville, OH: Gareth Stevens Publishing, 2003.

National Geographic. *United States Atlas for Young Explorers.* Washington, D.C.: National Geographic Children's Books, 2008.

Orr, Tamra B. *Alan Shepard.* New York, NY: Rosen Publishing Group, 2004.

Otfinoski, Steve. *New Hampshire.* Tarrytown, NY: Marshall Cavendish Benchmark, 2008.

Remini, Robert V. *Daniel Webster: The Man and His Time.* New York, NY: W. W. Norton and Company, 2009.

Remy, Richard C. *United States Government: Democracy in Action.* New York, NY: Glencoe McGraw-Hill, 2003.

Rosinsky, Nathalie M. *The Algonquin.* Mankato, MN: Compass Point Books, 2005.

Salinger, J. D. *The Catcher in the Rye.* Boston, MA: Little Brown, 1951.

Thomas, William David. *New Hampshire.* Strongsville, OH: Gareth Stevens Publishing, 2007.

BIBLIOGRAPHY

Abenaki Nation. "Darkness Falls." Retrieved January 20, 2010 (http://www.
    abenakination.org/darkness.html).

Concord Monitor. "New Hampshire's 2000s at a Glance." Retrieved January 18, 2010
    (http://www.concordmonitor.com/apps/pbcs.dll/article?AID=/20091231/
    NEWS01/912310301/1001/RSS01).

Dubois, Muriel L. *The States and Their Symbols.* Mankato, MN: Capstone Press, 2000.

Flow of History. "Native Americans in Vermont: The Abenaki." Retrieved
    January 20, 2010 (http://www.flowofhistory.org/themes/movement_settlement/
    abenaki.php).

JeanneShaheen.org. "More About Jeanne Shaheen." Retrieved July 24, 2009
    (http://www.jeanneshaheen.org/about/Jeanne-Shaheen-Extended-Bio).

MountWashington.org. "Frequently Asked Questions." Retrieved June 12, 2009
    (http://www.mountwashington.org/about/faq.php).

New Hampshire Department of Education. "About the Department of Education."
    Retrieved January 18, 2010 (http://www.ed.state.nh.us/education/doe/
    mission.htm).

New Hampshire Department of Environmental Services. "Environmental Fact Sheet:
    Global Climate Change and Its Impact on New Hampshire." Concord, NH:
    New Hampshire Department of Environmental Services, 2008.

New Hampshire Department of Environmental Services. "Environmental Fact Sheet:
    The New Hampshire Initiative to Restore Rivers Through Selective Dam Removal."
    Concord, NH: New Hampshire Department of Environmental Services, 2003.

New Hampshire Division of Forests and Lands. "NH State and Lands." Retrieved
    June 12, 2009 (http://www.nhdfl.org/new-hampshire-state-lands).

New Hampshire General Court. "State of New Hampshire House of Representatives."
    Retrieved, June 12, 2009 (http://www.gencourt.state.nh.us/house/default.htm).

New Hampshire Judicial Branch. "Judicial Branch: State of New Hampshire."
    Retrieved June 12, 2009 (http://www.courts.state.nh.us).

New Hampshire Senate. "History." Retrieved June 12, 2009 (http://www.gencourt.state.
    nh.us/senate/misc/history.html).

New Hampshire Senate. "How the Senate Operates." Retrieved June 12, 2009
    (http://www.gencourt.state.nh.us/senate/misc/business.html).

New Hampshire Timberland Owners Association. "About Us." Retrieved January 18,
    2010 (http://www.nhtoa.org/aboutus.html).

NH.com. "The Industrial Revolution in New Hampshire." Retrieved June 12, 2009
   (http://www.nh.com/apps/pbcs.dll/article?AID = /20060901/HISTORY07/
   309010009/-1/history).

NH.gov. "New Hampshire Almanac: A Brief History of New Hampshire." Retrieved
   June 12, 2009 (http://www.nh.gov/nhinfo/history.html).

NH.gov. "New Hampshire's Native American Heritage." Retrieved July 24, 2009
   (http://www.nh.gov/folklife/learning/traditions_native_americans.htm).

NH.gov. "State of New Hampshire: Executive Council." Retrieved June 12, 2009
   (http://www.nh.gov/council/index.html).

PortsmouthNH.com. "About Portsmouth & the Seacoast." Retrieved January 18, 2010
   (http://www.portsmouthnh.com/visitors/index.cfm).

Public Service of New Hampshire. "New Hampshire Fact Book: Taxes and Business
   Climate." Retrieved October 2, 2009 (http://www.psnh.com/SharePDFs/
   NHFactBook_TaxesandBusiness.pdf).

SHG Resources. "New Hampshire Firsts, Facts and Trivia." State Handbook & Guide.
   Retrieved September 4, 2009 (http://www.shgresources.com/nh/facts).

State of New Hampshire Judicial Branch. "Your Guide to the New Hampshire Courts."
   Concord, NH: New Hampshire Bar Association, 2008.

U.S. Census Bureau. "State and County Quick Facts: New Hampshire." Retrieved
   September 4, 2009 (http://quickfacts.census.gov/qfd/states/33000.html).

White House. "Presidents: Franklin Pierce." Retrieved June 12, 2009 (http://www.
   whitehouse.gov/about/presidents/FranklinPierce).

INDEX

About the Author

Lauren Ciarleglio is a writer from New York City. She studied journalism at Roger Williams University, where she received a B.A. in communications. Growing up in New England, Ciarleglio often traveled to New Hampshire with her family. This is her first book for Rosen Publishing.

Photo Credits

Cover (top left) Three Lions/Hulton Archive/Getty Images; cover (top right) © www.istockphoto.com/Denis Jr. Tangney; cover (bottom), pp. 9, 40 Shutterstock.com; pp. 3, 6, 12, 20, 25, 30, 38 Scientifica/Visuals Unlimited/Getty Images; p. 4 (top) © GeoAtlas; p. 7 Sandy Felsenthal/National Geographic/Getty Images; p. 11 © www.istockphoto.com/cjmckendry; p. 13 MPI/Hulton Archive/Getty Images; p. 15 © SuperStock; p. 17 Ohio Historical Society; p. 18 Walker Evans/Time & Life Pictures/Getty Images; pp. 21, 24 © AP Images; p. 26 © Richard Durnan/SuperStock; p. 29 Tyler Stableford/The Image Bank/Getty Images; p. 31 Elisabetta Villa/Getty Images; p. 34 Chip Somodevilla/Getty Images; p. 37 Library of Congress Prints and Photographs Division; p. 39 (left) Courtesy of Robesus, Inc.

Designer: Les Kanturek; Photo Researcher: Cindy Reiman